Marine Macrophytes of the Open-coast, Rocky Intertidal Habitats of the Cabrillo National Monument

Natural Resource Data Series NPS/MEDN/NRDS—2011/189

Steven N. Murray

Office of the Vice President for Academic Affairs
California State University, Fullerton
800 N. State College Blvd.
Fullerton, CA 92831-3599

Kathy Ann Miller

University Herbarium
1001 Valley Life Sciences Building #2465
University of California, Berkeley
Berkeley, California 94720

August 2011

U.S. Department of the Interior
National Park Service
Natural Resource Stewardship and Science
Fort Collins, Colorado

The National Park Service, Natural Resource Stewardship and Science office in Fort Colins, Colorado publishes a range of reports that address natural resource topics of interest and applicability to a broad audience in the National Park Service and others in natural resource management, including scientists, conservation and environmental constituencies, and the public.

The Natural Resource Data Series is intended for the timely release of basic data sets and data summaries. Care has been taken to assure accuracy of raw data values, but a thorough analysis and interpretation of the data has not been completed. Consequently, the initial analyses of data in this report are provisional and subject to change.

All manuscripts in the series receive the appropriate level of peer review to ensure that the information is scientifically credible, technically accurate, appropriately written for the intended audience, and designed and published in a professional manner.

Data in this report were collected and analyzed using methods based on established, peer-reviewed protocols and were analyzed and interpreted within the guidelines of the protocols.

Views, statements, findings, conclusions, recommendations, and data in this report do not necessarily reflect views and policies of the National Park Service, U.S. Department of the Interior. Mention of trade names or commercial products does not constitute endorsement or recommendation for use by the U.S. Government.

This report is available from the Mediterranean Coast Network (http://science.nature.nps.gov/im/units/medn/index.cfm) and the Natural Resource Publications Management website (http://www.nature.nps.gov/publications/nrpm/).

Please cite this publication as:

NPS 342/109342, August 2011

Contents

Figures

Tables

Abstract

The exposed, westward-facing rocky intertidal coast of the Cabrillo National Monument was thoroughly searched and all observed intertidal macrophytes recorded. A total of 94 marine algae and seagrasses (7 Chlorophyta, 19 Heterokontophyta - Class Phaeophyceae, 67 Rhodophyta, and 1 Spermatophyta) was identified. Conservatively, a minimum of 33 taxa (2 green, 5 brown, and 26 red seaweeds) had not been previously reported for the Cabrillo National Monument. The total number of taxa recorded was comparable to values obtained from prior intertidal studies in Monument waters and elsewhere in the southern California region. Of these 94 macrophytes, 51 (3 Chlorophyta, 11 Phaeophyceae, 36 Rhodophyta, and 1 Spermatophyta) were considered to be common to abundant on Monument shores based on subjective assessments of their occurrence within expected intertidal zones. The percentage (71.3% vs. 67.1%) of the rocky intertidal flora represented by red seaweeds was slightly greater than the percentage reported earlier for the rocky shore flora of the Southern California Bight. The percentage of green seaweeds (7.5% vs. 11.3%) was slightly lower while the percentage of brown seaweeds (20.2% vs. 20.7%) was nearly identical. Only a 72.3% overlap in species composition with central California was observed for the Cabrillo National Monument, a value similar to Santa Catalina and San Clemente Islands, indicating that this is one of the more warmer-water rocky intertidal floras in the Southern California Bight. The Cabrillo flora included 18 of 26 macrophyte species described as indicators of warmer water rocky shores in the Southern California Bight. At least three non-indigenous macrophytes were included in the Cabrillo National Monument flora. Given the unique biogeographic character and the documented impacts of public use of this southern part of the Point Loma Peninsula, we recommend that floristic surveys (and preferably ecological studies of distribution and abundance) be performed by skilled macrophyte taxonomists at least once every five years. This will be especially important for documenting likely changes in the intertidal macrophyte flora brought about by the introduction of non-indigenous species and on-going changes in ocean climate.

Acknowledgments

We are grateful for the field and laboratory assistance of several individuals but most notably Janine Kido, Aimee Bullard, and Lisa Gilbane. We also would like to thank Jayson Smith and Sean Vogt who assisted with the taking and preparation of the specimen photographs and Kelly Donovan who prepared Figure 1. We appreciate the efforts of Andrea Compton, Bonnie Becker, and Benjamin Pister from Natural Resource Science, Cabrillo National Monument, National Park Service who initiated this project and waited patiently for its completion. This study was funded by the National Park Service, Department of the Interior and was undertaken as part of the MARINe collaborative supported by the Pacific Outer Continental Shelf Region, Minerals Management Service (MMS), U. S. Department of the Interior. The views expressed herein do not necessarily reflect the views of any of these entities.

Note: The rights to all photographs are retained by Steven N. Murray (SNM); photographs cannot be reproduced in any form without the written consent of SNM. Exempt from this provision is the use of photographs by the Cabrillo National Monument or the National Park Service for educational use, including displays and brochures given that SNM is cited and credited.

Introduction

Originally established in 1913 as a small 0.4 hectare (1 acre) parcel to house a monument to Juan Rodriguez Cabrillo, the Cabrillo National Monument now occupies ca. 64.75 hectares (160 acres) of land and is responsible for the administration of 1.5 km of rocky intertidal habitat and 51.8 hectares (128 acres) of submerged land at the southern end of the Point Loma Peninsula in San Diego County, California (Figure 1). The Monument has been part of the National Park System since 1933 and is bordered to the west by the Pacific Ocean and to the east by San Diego Bay. The Marine Administrative Area extends 274.3 m (900 ft) seaward on the ocean side of the peninsula (McArdle 1997). Nested within the Marine Administrative Area is the Point Loma Reserve (now referred to as the Mia Tegner State Marine Conservation Area), which was established by the California Fish and Game Commission in 1978; the State Marine Conservation Area extends 45.7 m (150 ft) from the shoreline and occupies a shoreline distance of 1.13 km (0.7 mi) (McArdle 1997). Recreational and commercial fishing are allowed with some limitations within Monument administered waters but the take of invertebrates and marine plants has been prohibited at least since the late 1970s.

Besides its statue of Juan Rodriguez Cabrillo, restored lighthouse, and spectacular visitor center, grounds and views of San Diego Bay, the Cabrillo National Monument has become known for its rich and diverse rocky intertidal communities along the ocean-facing south end of the Point Loma coastline. The Monument contains the only public access to the open coast shoreline on the southern end of the peninsula and has long been a favored site for visitors seeking to observe coastal marine life. It is estimated that each year about 10% of the approximately one million visitors to the Cabrillo National Monument also visit the Monument's rocky shores (Engle and Largier 2006). The individual and cumulative activities of this large number of shore visitors have been of concern for years and have led to past studies to detect visitor impacts (e.g., Zedler 1976, 1978) and monitoring programs designed to determine the dynamics of key species populations (e.g., Engle and Davis 2000a,b; Engle et al. 2000, Engle 2005). Other recent studies of the Cabrillo National Monument include an assessment of coastal water resources and watershed conditions (Engle and Largier 2006) and the development of a checklist of shore fishes (Craig and Pondella 2006).

Because of its popularity, a major goal of the Cabrillo National Monument has been to improve understanding of the impacts of regional human activities, including public visitation, so as to manage the shoreline and tidepools in ways that ensure public access and enjoyment while protecting the rich diversity of marine life. Macroalgae and seagrasses are ecologically important components of temperate rocky intertidal communities throughout the world. These macrophytes contribute to coastal productivity and provide habitat for invertebrates and fishes. Therefore, an inventory of the macrophyte resources of the shores administered by the Cabrillo National Monument is of importance to Park managers. This report follows previous surveys of rocky intertidal and other natural resources and adds to our understanding of the ecological communities of the Cabrillo National Monument by providing an updated list of those marine macroalgae and seagrasses found in intertidal waters on the Monument's heavily-visited, western facing coast.

Methods

The westward-facing, open coast, rocky intertidal habitats of the Cabrillo National Monument (Figure 1) are characterized by poorly-consolidated, gently sloping sedimentary rocky reefs projecting out from eroding sandstone cliffs; scattered rocks and boulders occur on top of the relatively flat rocky surfaces (Engle et al. 2000). Park managers have divided this Monument shoreline into three zones (Zones I-III) for purposes of limiting and assessing visitor activities.

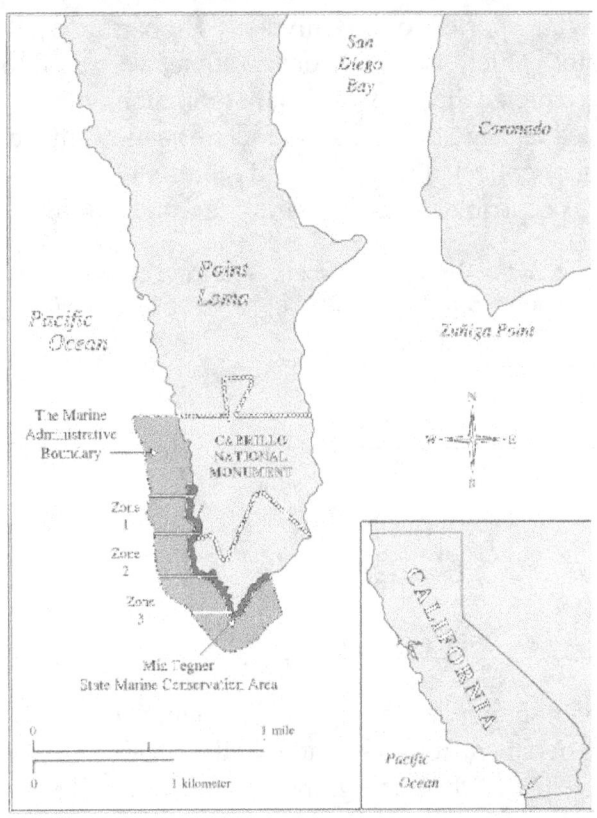

Figure 1. The Cabrillo National Monument study area on the western-facing, southern Point Loma coastline. Shown are the Marine Administrative Area and the Mia Tegner State Marine Conservation Area where restrictions on extraction occur. Zones I, II, and III were designated by Park Managers.

The boundaries and locations of these zones are described by Engle et al. (2000) as follows. Zone I includes the intertidal habitat ranging from ca. 220 m north to ca. 110 m south of the main access point to the shoreline. Zone II continues south along the peninsula and encompasses about 330 m of shoreline. Zone III extends another 330 m to the south tip of Point Loma. Zone III, which is dominated by broad, flat, rocky reefs and shallow pools, was closed to the public in 1996 to protect its biological resources and to serve as a control area for assessing visitor impacts. The intertidal shore extent increases in length from north to south along this portion of the peninsula, varying from 20 to 40 m in Zone I to greater than 70 m in Zone III. A similar gradient in wave exposure occurs with Zone I receiving more wave energy than Zone III (Engle et al. 2000).

3

The accessible rocky intertidal habitats of all three zones were visited during low tide periods on January 24, March 9-10, and June 28, 2005 (Table 1). The shoreline was thoroughly searched and all observed intertidal macrophytes recorded; drift specimens, when observed, were also noted and collected. Field notes were taken and qualitative estimates of the abundances of intertidal taxa were made. Searches began several hours before low tide maxima and concluded either when shoreline access was restricted by advancing tides or diminishing daylight. Attempts were made to collect specimens of all observed macrophytes. Some material was made into herbarium specimens in the field while other samples were preserved for later examination and specimen preparation. All collected materials were transported to the University Herbarium at the University of California Berkeley for further study. Field notes and observations were used to make annotations of observed macrophytes and to indicate the more abundant (common within their expected intertidal habitat) taxa. Thus, reported data are based on field identifications made by the authors and by further laboratory inspection of collected materials and represent the common rocky intertidal seaweeds and sea grasses occurring at the site during the study period.

Table 1. Low-tide Conditions During Macrophyte Surveys of the Westward Facing Shoreline of the Cabrillo National Monument. Listed Conditions are Predictions for Point Loma, California based on NOAA Tidal Data.

Date	Low Tide Amplitude (ft) with Respect to MLLW	Time (hrs)
January 24, 2005	-0.8	15:15
March 9, 2005	-1.4	14:44
March 10, 2005	-1.0	15:16
June 28, 2005	+0.5	09:21

In addition to field collections and observations, photographs were taken of 72 abundant and conspicuous macrophytes using mostly specimens obtained from elsewhere in the Southern California region. Therefore, although the morphologies of the photographed seaweeds are representative of species found in the Cabrillo National Monument, the photographs do not serve as samples of macrophytes actually collected from the Monument shoreline.

The method employed in this study is described as a coarse scale survey (Murray et al. 2006), a technique commonly used to build inventories of macrophytes on rocky shores and to make qualitative estimates of abundance. Surveys such as these tend to capture the vast majority of species present when performed by experienced investigators. Exceptions are crustose species, which are usually under-represented in field surveys because complete identification is time-consuming and frequently cannot be made without reproductive material. In addition, small, filamentous and rare seaweeds often escape detection. Additional site searches and collections performed during different periods of the year and more detailed work on crustose and smaller macrophytes would be expected to increase the number of taxa occupying the Cabrillo National Monument shoreline.

Results

A total of 94 macrophytes was recorded growing on the exposed, westward-facing rocky intertidal coast of the Cabrillo National Monument, including 7 Chlorophyta, 19 Heterokontophyta (Class Phaeophyceae), 67 Rhodophyta, and 1 Spermatophyta. Additional species of brown (3) and red (2) seaweeds were collected exclusively as drift specimens washed up from adjacent subtidal habitats. Of these 94 intertidal macrophytes, 51 taxa (3 Chlorophyta, 11 Phaeophyceae, 36 Rhodophyta, and 1 Spermatophyta) were considered to be common to abundant on Monument shores during the sampling periods based on subjective assessments of their occurrence within expected intertidal zones. The additional 43 macrophytes were rare, meaning that few specimens were observed during our searches.

Table 2. Common macrophytes of the open-coast, rocky intertidal shoreline of the Cabrillo National Monument, Point Loma, California. Excluded are full inventories of crustose and smaller, filamentous algae which escaped detection during site searches. Five taxa were also collected exclusively as drift specimens: *Cryptopleura ruprechtiana* (J. Agardh) Kylin [*Botryoglossum farlowianum* (J.Agardh) DeToni], *Leptocladia binghamiae* J. Agardh, *Macrocystis pyrifera* (L.) C. Agardh, *Pelagophycus porra* (Leman) Setchell, and *Pterygophora californica* Ruprecht. Note: annotations include comparisons with previous macrophyte lists compiled for the Cabrillo National Monument by Zedler (1976, 1978). Zones refer to subdivisions of the open coast, westward-facing intertidal habitat established by site managers (see Figure 1).

Macrophyte Taxa	Annotations
Chlorophyta	
+*Bryopsis pennata* var. *minor* J. Agardh	[*Bryopsis pennatula* J. Agardh] Encountered once in a pool in the low zone (Zone II). It was listed in Zedler (1978) as *Bryopsis pinnatula*.
*+*Chaetomorpha aerea* (Dillwyn) Kützing (Plate 1)	[*Chaetomorpha linum* (Müller) Kützing according to some authors] Straight green filaments lining shallow pools, middle zone.
#*Chaetomorpha spiralis* Okamura (Plate 2)	Not reported in Zedler (1976, 1978). Epiphytic on other seaweeds and *Phyllospadixi* in the low zone, (Zones I and III). Bright green, curling and spiraling around host axes.
+*Cladophora microcladioides* Collins	Encountered once, in a pool in the low zone (Zone III). This may be one of the species listed in Zedler (1976) as *Cladophora* spp.; it is small, with conspicuous pectinate (unilateral) branching.

*Common to abundant species in expected intertidal habitats.
+Taxa described by Abbott and Hollenberg (1976) to occur along the central California coast north of Point Conception. [Note: *Caulacanthus ustulatus*, which was not listed in Abbott and Hollenberg (1976), is included in this group of species.]
#Taxa found south but not north of Point Conception based on Abbott and Hollenberg's distributional records.

Table 2. Common macrophytes of the open-coast, rocky intertidal shoreline of the Cabrillo National Monument, Point Loma, California (continued).

Macrophyte Taxa	Annotations
+*Codium fragile* ssp. *californicum* (J. Agardh) Maggs (Plate 3)	[*Codium fragile* (Suringar) Hariot] Occasional on the tops and sides of boulders in the low zone. This is the sole species of *Codium* observed at the Cabrillo National Monument site.
*+*Ulva* spp. [*Enteromorpha* spp.] (Plate 4)	Several small tubular ulvoids occur in the high zone on the damp faces of sandstone boulders and cliffs. They are especially prominent in Zones I and II. Our samples are unbranched and compressed. One is larger (1 cm) and dark green; the other is smaller (5 mm) and light green. Both aggregate to form patches or fringes. This complex may include what was listed in Zedler (1976) as *Enteromorpha flexuosa* (now *Ulva flexuosa* Wulfen).
*+*Ulva californica* Wille (Plate 5)	Forming turfs on the surface of upper and middle zone rocks, possibly in response to disturbance. *Ulva angusta*, listed in Zedler (1976), is considered a synonym of *Ulva californica*. We did not observe specimens that we identified as *Ulva rigida*, which was listed in Zedler (1978). This genus in California needs work, including molecular data.

Heterokontophyta (Class Phaeophyceae)

Macrophyte Taxa	Annotations
#*Colpomenia sinuosa* (Mertens ex Roth) Derbès & Solier (Plate 6)	Most common species of *Colpomenia* at the study site. Growing mostly on coralline turf.
#*Colpomenia tuberculata* Saunders (Plate 7)	Not reported in Zedler (1976, 1978). Occasional in Zones II and III; epiphytic on coralline turf. Distinctive thick, warty thallus
#*Dictyopteris undulata* Holmes (Plate 8)	Occasional in low zone pools.
*+*Dictyota coriacea* (Holmes) Hwang, H.S. Kim & W.J. Lee (Plate 9)	[*Pachydictyon coriaceum* (Holmes) Okamura] This species and *Taonia lennebackerae* are the most common members of the Dictyotales at the site. We found a few small specimens resembling *Dictyota flabellata* that were probably young *D. coriacea*.
*+*Egregia menziesii* (Turner) Areschoug (Plate 10)	Low zone, and in drift.
+*Eisenia arborea* Areschoug (Plate 11)	Juveniles occurred occasionally in low pools; adult thalli in drift.

Table 2. Common macrophytes of the open-coast, rocky intertidal shoreline of the Cabrillo National Monument, Point Loma, California (continued).

Macrophyte Taxa	Annotations
*#*Endarachne binghamiae* J. Agardh (Plate 12)	Narrow thalli were common in the high zone, on cliff and boulder faces and scattered through the middle zone. The medulla of a few wider specimens was checked to be sure that they were not *Petalonia fascia*; they were not.
*+*Petrospongium rugosum* (Okamura) Setchell & Gardner (Plate 13)	[*Cylindrocarpus rugosus* Okamura]. Growing on horizontal and vertical rock surfaces in the mid zone. Listed in Zedler (1976).
*+*Pseudolithoderma nigrum* Hollenberg (Plate 14)	[*Pseudolithoderma nigra* Hollenberg] Not reported in Zedler (1976, 1978) lists, but certainly present at that time. This is a black, extensive/irregular, tightly adherent, thin crust that is common in the barnacle zone.
*+*Ralfsia* spp (Plate 15)	This represents a complex of brown crustose species, some of which are likely the alternate stage of upright phases (e.g., *Scytosiphon lomentaria*). We observed light brown and chocolate brown crusts.
#*Sargassum agardhianum* Farlow (Plate 16)	Infrequent, Zones II-III. This species is highly seasonal, eroding back during the winter and growing in the late spring-summer. Not reported in Zedler (1976, 1978).
*+*Sargassum muticum* (Yendo) Fenscholt (Plate 17)	Common in middle and low pools. This species is also seasonal, growing during the winter and eroding back to holdfasts in late summer-fall. It is a non-native. It was reported from Quivera Basin, Mission Bay in 1958-59 (Stewart 1991). This could represent a separate introduction from the Puget Sound introduction described in Abbott and Hollenberg (1976).
+*Scytosiphon dotyi* Wynne (Plate 18)	Narrow tubular, unbranched thalli in small clusters in the upper zone, on cliff faces. Not reported in Zedler (1976, 1978).
*+*Silvetia compressa* (J. Agardh) Serrão, Cho, Boo & Brawley (Plate 19)	[*Pelvetia fastigiata* (J. Agardh) DeToni] Forming canopies on middle zone rocks. Important habitat engineer and susceptible to trampling damage.
*#*Sphacelaria californica* Sauvageau	Common on rock in shallow middle zone pools. This, the larger of the two species found at the site (tufts > 1 cm), can be conspicuous. Not reported in Zedler (1976, 1978).

Table 2. Common macrophytes of the open-coast, rocky intertidal shoreline of the Cabrillo National Monument, Point Loma, California (continued).

Macrophyte Taxa	Annotations
+*Sphacelaria rigidula* Kützing	[*Sphacelaria furcigera* Kützing] This species is epiphytic, forming small (< 1 cm) tufts of filaments, usually on corallines. *Sphacelaria didichotoma* was listed in Zedler (1978); this report may well have represented *S. rigidula*, which is far more common in intertidal habitats (Stewart 1991).
*#*Stephanocystis dioica* (Gardner) Draisma, Ballesteros, Rousseau, & Thibaut (Plate 20)	[*Halidrys dioica* Gardner] Some may confuse the vegetative portion of this species with *Stepanocystis* species previously referred to the genus *Cystoseira* , although *S. dioica* typically occurs in the low intertidal while the *"Cystoseira"* spp. are more characteristic of the shallow subtidal zone. We observed neither *S. osmundacea* nor *S. setchellii* in our surveys, although they may occur in water deeper than where we worked. The former was listed in Zedler (1976) and the latter in Zedler (1978).
*#*Taonia lennebackerae* J. Agardh (Plate 21)	Listed as rare in Zedler (1976); frequent in 2005. Its occurrence is related to sand movement, so its populations may fluctuate year to year (Stewart 1991).
#*Zonaria farlowii* Setchell & Gardner (Plate 22)	Not reported in Zedler (1976, 1978). We found a single specimen in a low intertidal pool, although we expected to see more since *Z. farlowii* occurs in sand-influenced sites, as does *Taonia*.

Rhodophyta

*+*Acrosorium ciliolatum* (Harvey) Kylin (Plate 23)	[*Acrosorium uncinatum* (Turner) Kylin, *Acrosorium venulosum* (Zanardini) Kylin]. Epiphytic on other seaweeds, and on rock, low zone and in drift.
+*Ahnfeltiopsis leptophylla* P.C. Silva & DeCew	[*Gymnogongrus leptophyllus* J. Agardh] Not reported in Zedler (1976, 1978). Occasional in sandy pools.
#*Amphiroa beauvoisii* Lamouroux (Plate 24)	[*Amphiroa zonata* Yendo] Not reported in Zedler (1976, 1978). Rare; one specimen observed in Zone II. Terete intergenicula, dichotomous branching. More common in warm-water years (Stewart 1991).

Table 2. Common macrophytes of the open-coast, rocky intertidal shoreline of the Cabrillo National Monument, Point Loma, California (continued).

Macrophyte Taxa	Annotations
+*Bangia vermicularis* Harvey	[*Bangia fusco-purpurea* (Dillwyn) Lyngbye] Not reported in Zedler (1976, 1978). Fine dark red to brown-black hair-like thalli plastered in patches to upper zone rock walls. This species is a winter-spring annual in San Diego County (Stewart 1991).
*+Bossiella dichotoma (Manza) P.C. Silva (Plate 25)	[*Bossiella orbigniana* ssp. *dichotoma* (Manza) Johansen] Frequent in the low zone and subtidal (common in drift). These thalli are almost strictly dichotomous with a zig-zag outline – sharply pointed with gaps between successive intergenicula. Stewart (1991) does not report *B. orbigniana* ssp. *dichotoma* (*B. dichotoma*) from San Diego County.
+*Callophyllis violacea* J. Agardh	Not reported in Zedler (1976, 1978). Small thalli, usually epiphytic on corallines in the low zone. More common in the subtidal zone. We observed no other species in the genus *Callophyllis*. Stewart (1991) reports only one subtidal specimen of *Callophyllis firma* (listed in Zedler 1976); she says that small, peltate subtidal thalli represent germlings of *Callophyllis flabellulata* or species in the Rhodymeniaceae. We cannot evaluate the Zedler (1976) report of *Callophyllis firma* in the absence of a voucher specimen.
*+Caulacanthus ustulatus (Mertens ex Turner) Kützing (Plate 26)	Not reported in Zedler (1976, 1978); not in Abbott and Hollenberg (1976). Common in the upper zones and into the middle zone. Creeping, terete, brick-red axes with short pointed branches. This species, which is believed to be an introduction, is becoming increasingly common in southern California and was recently observed in central and northern California.
*+Centroceras clavulatum (C. Agardh) Montagne (Plate 27)	Common constituent of middle zone turf.
#*Ceramium sinicola* Setchell & Gardner (Plate 28)	Not reported in Zedler (1976, 1978). Epiphytic on *Codium fragile*; fully corticated.
*+Chondracanthus canaliculatus (Harvey) Guiry in Hommersand, Guiry, Fredericq & Leister (Plate 29)	[*Gigartina canaliculata* Harvey] Occasional, usually small thalli, in middle zone, especially under *Silvetia* and in pools and crevices.

Table 2. Common macrophytes of the open-coast, rocky intertidal shoreline of the Cabrillo National Monument, Point Loma, California (continued).

Macrophyte Taxa	Annotations
*+*Chondracanthus spinosus* (Kützing) Guiry in Hommersand, Guiry, Fredericq & Leister (Plate 30)	[*Gigartina spinosa* (Kützing) Harvey] Not reported in Zedler (1976, 1978). Frequent, mostly under canopy of *Silvetia* or sides of rocks or in pools in middle and low zone. Stewart (1991) considers this species, in its many forms, common in San Diego County (as did Dawson), while *C. tepida*, which it may resemble, is rare and inconspicuous. In the Herbarium of the Allan Hancock Foundation (now in the U.C. Berkeley herbarium), there are many specimens of *G. tepida* from the Gulf of California, but only 5 from California (Balboa Harbor, Orange County and the Long Beach breakwater). It is difficult to evaluate the Zedler (1976) report of *C. tepida* (as *Gigartina tepida*) without a voucher specimen.
#*Chondria acrorhizophora* Setchell & Gardner (Plate 31)	[*Chondria californica* (Collins) Kylin] Epiphytic on *Phyllospadix*.
+*Chondria* sp.	We agree with Zedler (1976) and Stewart (1991): Species in *Chondria* (*C. dasyphylla, C. oppositoclada, C. nidifica*) are difficult to distinguish.
*+*Chondria nidifica* Harvey	This robust and distinctive species is frequent in the low zone.
*+*Corallina chilensis* Decaisne (Plate 32)	[*Corallina officinalis* var. *chilensis* (Decaisne) Kützing] Occasional to common; low zone.
*#*Corallina pinnatifolia* (Manza) Dawson (Plate 33)	This very abundant and polymorphic species, the foundation of the middle and low zone turfs, likely includes *C. polysticha* and *C. frondescens*, both listed in Zedler (1976) and Stewart (1991).
*+*Corallina vancouveriensis* Yendo (Plate 34)	Part of the coralline turf, middle and low zones.
*+*Corallophila eatoniana* (Farlow) T.O. Cho, Choi, G.I. Hansen & Boo (Plate 35)	[*Ceramium eatonianum* (Farlow) DeToni] Common along the edges of pools in middle zone turf.

Table 2. Common macrophytes of the open-coast, rocky intertidal shoreline of the Cabrillo National Monument, Point Loma, California (continued).

Macrophyte Taxa	Annotations
*+*Cryptopleura corallinara* (Nott) Gardner / *Cryptopleura crispa* Kylin (Plate 36)	These species are very similar, both epiphytic on corallines and other seaweeds, with thin blades, microscopic veins, ruffled margins and tetrasporangia borne on the margins or on marginal proliferations (Stewart 1991). The type localities of both species are in San Diego County; *C. corallinara* is the older epithet. *C. rosacea* was listed in Zedler (1978). Stewart (1991) says "…specimens similar to the forms described for *C. rosacea* are occasionally found; the collections we have seen probably represent dense clumps of *C. crispa*. Published records for *C. rosacea* refer only to drift specimens at Carmel in central California."
*+*Cryptopleura violacea* (J. Agardh) Kylin (Plate 37)	Epiphytic, but narrower, linear (ribbon-like), and lacking a ruffled margin (compared to *Cryptopleura corallinara /Cryptopleura crispa)*. However, Abbott and Hollenberg (1976) mention that this species is "perhaps not clearly distinct from *C. crispa*". This complex needs work!
+*Cumagloia andersonii* (Farlow) Setchell & Gardner (Plate 38)	In patches, on tops of boulders in the high zone (Zone I). In Zedler (1976), it was listed as occurring in the low intertidal in *Phyllospadix* pools, a very anomalous habitat. This report may be in error.
#*Dasya binghamiae* A.J.K. Millar	[*Pogonophorella californica* (J. Agardh) P.C. Silva] Occasional under *Phyllospadix*, in sand. Not reported in Zedler (1976, 1978).
*+*Erythrocystis saccata* (J. Agardh) Silva (Plate 39)	On *Laurencia pacifica*.
+*Erythroglossum californicum* (J. Agardh) J. Agardh	[*Anisocladella pacifica* Kylin] In *Phyllospadix* pools, in sand. Not reported in Zedler (1976, 1978).
*+*Gastroclonium compressum* (Hollenberg) Chang & Xia (Plate 40)	[*Coeloseira compressa* Hollenberg] *Gastroclonium parvum* (Hollenberg) Chang & Xia [*Coeloseira parva* Hollenberg] We found it difficult to distinguish these species. Frequent, often with a whitish iridescence; epiphytic on the middle and low turfs.
*+*Gelidium coulteri* Harvey (Plate 41)	Small thalli, in crevices and pools in the upper zone, and scattered into the middle zone. This species was added to the list in Zedler (1978).

11

Table 2. Common macrophytes of the open-coast, rocky intertidal shoreline of the Cabrillo National Monument, Point Loma, California (continued).

Macrophyte Taxa	Annotations
Gelidium purpurascens Gardner (Plate 42)	Not reported in Zedler (1976, 1978). Could be confused with *G. robustum*, which is generally larger, with large apices and naked lower axes. Low zone.
*+*Gelidium pusillum* (Stackhouse) LeJolie (Plate 43)	This is a provisional determination for this constituent of the middle zone turf.
+*Gelidium robustum* (Gardner) Hollenberg & Abbott (Plate 44)	Occasional in the low zone and in the drift.
+*Gymnogongrus chiton* (Howe) P.C. Silva & DeCew in Silva	[*Gymnogongrus platyphyllus* Gardner] Not reported in Zedler (1976, 1978). Flat, broad, dichotomous axes, with conspicuous nemathecia (fertile bumps); low zone.
*#*Haliptilon roseum* (Lamarck) D.J. Garbary & H.W. Johansen (Plate 45)	[*Haliptilon gracile* (Lamouroux) Johansen] In pools, low zone.
+*Herposiphonia verticillata* (Harvey) Kylin	Epiphytic on corallines and other seaweeds, low zone turf.
#*Heterosiphonia erecta* Gardner	Not reported in Zedler (1976, 1978). Occasional epiphyte, middle and low zones.
*+*Hildenbrandia* sp. (Plate 46)	Uncalcified, dark red crusts, especially in upper pools.
*#*Hypnea valentiae* (Turner) Montagne (Plate 47)	With spiny, terete (cylindrical) axes; abundant between June and October (Stewart 1991). *H. johnstonii* was listed in Zedler (1978); it has not been found in San Diego County, according to Stewart (1991).
#*Hypnea variabilis* Okamura	With narrow, flattened (compressed) axes. Considered rare by Stewart (1991).
*#*Jania crassa* Lamouroux (Plate 48)	Occasional in pools, middle and low zones. We would expect to see *Jania tenella,* listed in Zedler (1976), as well but did not during these surveys.
*#*Laurencia masonii* Setchell & Gardner (Plate 49)	Stewart (1991) includes this species in her circumscription of *L. pacifica.* We distinguish *L. masonii* on the basis of its longer, less branched/congested branches, especially in the lower portion. Its anatomy (medullary thickenings) is distinctive in some cases. Not reported in Zedler (1976, 1978).

Table 2. Common macrophytes of the open-coast, rocky intertidal shoreline of the Cabrillo National Monument, Point Loma, California (continued).

Macrophyte Taxa	Annotations
*+*Laurencia pacifica* Kylin (Plate 50)	Common in the middle and low zones.
*+*Laurencia subopposita* (J. Agardh) Setchell (Plate 51)	Occasional, on other seaweeds and *Phyllospadix*; low zone.
+*Leptocladia binghamiae* J. Agardh	Collected in the drift.
*+*Lithophyllum neofarlowii* Setchell & Mason (Plate 52)	[*Pseudolithophyllum neofarlowii* (Setch. & Mason) W.H. Adey] Not reported in Zedler (1976, 1978) but probably present. Pale lavender calcified crust, growing in upper zone tide pools and crevices.
*+*Lithothrix aspergillum* Gray (Plate 53)	Occasional in pools and turf, low zone.
*#*Lomentaria hakodatensis* Yendo (Plate 54)	Not reported in Zedler (1976, 1978). However, the description of *Binghamia californica* in the Zedler (1978) list is very similar to that of *Lomentaria* and does not resemble *B. californica*, which, according to Stewart (1991), does not occur in San Diego County. *Binghamia forkii* is reported to be common in the San Diego area (Stewart 1991), but this species is conspicuously flattened rather than filiform, as is stated in the Zedler (1978) description. We did not encounter *Binghamia*. Pink-orange tubular thalli without septa, irregularly branched but often with apices shaped like saguaro cacti. Tiny, creeping, epiphytic on middle zone algal turfs. Non-native.
+*Mazzaella affinis* (Harvey) Fredericq in Hommersand, Guiry, Fredericq & Leister (Plate 55)	[*Rhodoglossum affine* (Harvey) Kylin] Small thalli, occasional at the bases of boulders, in crevices, middle and low zones.
+*Mazzaella leptorhynchos* (J. Agardh) Leister in Hommersand, Guiry, Fredericq & Leister (Plate 56)	[*Gigartina leptorhynchos* J. Agardh] Mostly small thalli, occasional at the bases of boulders, in crevices, middle and low zones.
*+*Melobesia marginata* Setchell & Foslie (see Plate 57)	Not reported in Zedler (1976, 1978). Small, calcified crusts on low zone species, especially *Osmundea*.
+*Neogastroclonium subarticulatum* (Turner) L. Le Gall, Dalen & G. W. Saunders (Plate 58)	[*Gastroclonium coulteri* (Harvey) Kylin] Occasional, in pools in low zone.
*+*Nienburgia andersoniana* (J. Agardh) Kylin (Plate 59)	Not reported in Zedler (1976, 1978). Low zone; creeping, forming upright thin pink blades with distinct midribs and dentate margins.

Table 2. Common macrophytes of the open-coast, rocky intertidal shoreline of the Cabrillo National Monument, Point Loma, California (continued).

Macrophyte Taxa	Annotations
#*Ophiocladus simpliciusculus* (Crouan & Crouan) Falkenberg	Not reported in Zedler (1976, 1978). Part of the mixture of epiphytic filaments (with *Polysiphonia*, *Herposiphonia*, *Centroceras*), occurring in the middle and low zone turfs. Resembles *Polysiphonia* but with 16-18 pericentral cells and 2-3 tetrasporangia per segment.
*#*Osmundea sinicola* (Setchell & Gardner) Nam (Plate 60)	[*Laurencia sinicola* Setchell & Gardner] Common in the middle zone turf.
#*Osmundea spectabilis* var. *diegoensis* (Dawson) Nam (Plate 61)	[*Laurencia spectabilis* var. *diegoensis* Dawson] *O. spectabilis* exhibits a morphological cline from north to south. Most specimens (including our vouchers) fit the description of var. *diegoensis*, with narrow, irregular thalli, but some grade into *O. spectabilis* var. *spectabilis* (Postels & Ruprecht) Nam, a form common in the north and in upwelling areas south of Point Conception.
*+*Plocamium pacificum* Kylin (Plate 62)	[*Plocamium cartilagineum* (Linnaeus) P.S. Dixon; *Plocamium cartilagineum* ssp. *pacificum* Silva] Frequent in *Phyllospadix* pools.
+*Polysiphonia scopulorum* var. *villum* (J. Agardh) Hollenberg	Not reported in Zedler (1976, 1978). Forming short velvety mats on rock in the middle zone.
*+*Polysiphonia* spp. (Plate 63)	At least two other species of *Polysiphonia* are present, but were not identified in the absence of voucher specimens.
+*Porphyra perforata* J. Agardh (Plate 64)	Not reported in Zedler (1976, 1978). Small blades growing on rock in the upper zone. *Porphyrella californica* was listed in Zedler (1978) as growing on "upper intertidal barnacle rocks" in the spring of 1977. This species, occurring on mussels and gooseneck barnacles, was tentatively identified in areas where *P. perforata* grew on rocks in San Diego County by Stewart (1991). The specimens reported in Zedler (1978), growing on rock, may represent *P. perforata*.
+*Prionitis lanceolata* (Harvey) Harvey (Plate 65)	In low pools and subtidal (in drift). Polymorphic.

Table 2. Common macrophytes of the open-coast, rocky intertidal shoreline of the Cabrillo National Monument, Point Loma, California (continued).

Macrophyte Taxa	Annotations
#*Prionitis linearis* Kylin	[*Prionitis angustata* (Okamura) Okamura] Not reported in Zedler (1976, 1978). Resembles *Carpopeltis*, but with broader axes, not crisped. Regularly dichotomous, dark brown-red, flattened axes, short internodes; low zone. This fits the description in Abbott and Hollenberg (1976), but is not the *P. angustata* of Japan. It is a recognizable entity throughout the Southern California Bight, especially in warmer parts (including islands).
*#*Pterocladiella capillacea* (S.G.Gmelin) Santelices & Hommersand (Plate 66)	[*Pterocladia capillacea* (S.G. Gmelin) Bornet] Common in middle zone pools, under *Silvetia* and in the low zone.
+*Pterosiphonia baileyi* (Harvey) Falkenberg (Plate 67)	Occasional in the low zone.
*+*Pterosiphonia dendroidea* (Montagne) Falkenberg (Plate 68)	Inconspicuous but frequent, especially associated with *Phyllospadix* and middle-low zone turf.
+*Rhodymenia californica* Kylin (Plate 69)	Narrow, regularly dichotomous blades. Low zone, on the shaded sides of boulders.
+*Rhodymenia pacifica* Kylin (Plate 70)	Broader blades, blunt apices; low zone, on the shaded sides of boulders.
+*Schizymenia pacifica* (Kylin) Kylin	Not reported in Zedler (1976, 1978). Single specimen from face of boulder on the southern edge of Zone I, low. Slippery, brown-red, entire blade, without a stipe. Gland cells evident as tiny bright spots with hand lens.
+*Scinaia confusa* (Setchell) Huisman	[*Pseudogloiophloea confusa* (Setchell) Levring] Not reported in Zedler (1976, 1978). Single specimen collected in low pool in Zone I. Small, regularly dichotomous, tubular thallus, dark red.
+*Smithora naiadum* (Anderson) Hollenberg (Plate 71)	Reduced to small brown basal cushions in some seasons.
*#*Spyridia filamentosa* (Wulfen) Harvey	Not reported in Zedler (1976, 1978). Patchy but locally abundant, especially in warm-water periods (Stewart 1991). Deep red, fuzzy-looking because of abundant, short branches.
*+*Tiffaniella snyderae* (Farlow) Abbott	Not reported in Zedler (1976, 1978). Frequent in filamentous patches in *Phyllospadix* pools or as an epiphyte in middle and low turfs.

Table 2. Common macrophytes of the open-coast, rocky intertidal shoreline of the Cabrillo National Monument, Point Loma, California (continued).

Macrophyte Taxa	Annotations
Spermatophyta	
*+*Phyllospadix torreyi* Watson (Plate 72)	With narrow (1 mm wide) leaves. Common in low pools; with characteristic epiphytes (*Smithora*, *Melobesia*). Probably listed as *Phyllospadix scouleri* in Zedler (1976,1978) reports. Stewart (1991) says that *P. torrey* alone dominates between Ocean Beach and Point Loma. We did not observe inflorescences (flower stalks) which are diagnostic.

*Common to abundant species in expected intertidal habitats.
+Taxa described by Abbott and Hollenberg (1976) to occur along the central California coast north of Point Conception. [Note: *Caulacanthus ustulatus*, which was not listed in Abbott and Hollenberg (1976), is included in this group of species.]
#Taxa found south but not north of Point Conception based on Abbott and Hollenberg's distributional records.

Discussion

The number of taxa we recorded for Cabrillo National Monument waters was comparable to values reported from prior studies performed in Monument waters and elsewhere in the southern California region. Previous records of the macrophyte flora of the Cabrillo National Monument are contained in Zedler (1976, 1978) and Engle (2005). In 1976, Zedler reported on transect studies to document the ecological resources of the rocky intertidal habitats within Monument jurisdiction. Later, Zedler (1978) examined public use effects in the Cabrillo National Monument intertidal zone. In these reports, the species and taxa observed were listed; however, several records were listed as unknown or identified only to genus; in addition, some identifications (e.g., *Analipus japonicus*) were questionable. We combined the records from the two reports to create a 1976-78 flora for the study site after eliminating unknowns and highly questionable identifications, making currently accepted taxonomic combinations, and updating nomenclature. This produced a flora of 101 macrophytes for the Zedler studies, a number highly comparable to the 94 reported for our intertidal surveys. Engle (2005) listed 86 macrophyte taxa from the same area based on data for intertidal transect sampling reported by field researchers from the University of California Santa Cruz. These records also contained several taxa combinations and identifications only to the genus or form (e.g., crustose seaweeds) level of taxonomic discrimination.

Our floristic records for the Cabrillo National Monument are comparable to records for other rocky intertidal floras in the region. For example, Murray and Littler (1989) reported an average of 76 taxa for 21 sites distributed throughout the Southern California Bight based mostly on quadrat samples distributed over a much more limited rocky intertidal area at each site than that examined during our study. For the 12 of these 21 sites that were sampled multiple times, the average number of taxa recorded was 84.8. One of these sites, Ocean Beach (32° 44' 35" N; 117° 15' 15" W), is in San Diego County on the north end of the Point Loma Peninsula. This site was found to have a macrophyte flora consisting of 80 taxa (Murray and Littler 1989). In contrast, the number of conspicuous macrophytes (22 to 47) recorded for one-time surveys of five sites on the Palos Verdes Peninsula (Gerrard 2005) were much lower than those observed at the Cabrillo National Monument. Unlike this study and those of Murray and Littler (1989), Gerrard's surveys included only conspicuous species recorded from the intertidal zone from high to low water. Gerrard's study sites were those originally established by Dawson (1959, 1965) and only "conspicuous" taxa were recorded in order to produce comparable data to those obtained by Dawson. Thus, the number of taxa recorded during our study would be expected to be greater than numbers reported by Gerrard (2005) for Dawson's Palos Verdes sites regardless of the actual floral richness. This underscores the importance of sampling or collection methods and the level and quality of taxonomic discrimination in comparing floral richness among sites.

Rocky intertidal floras in the Southern California Bight are numerically dominated by red seaweeds as was the case for the Cabrillo National Monument. We observed the percentage of the Cabrillo National Monument rocky intertidal flora represented by red seaweeds to be 71.3%, a value a little higher than the percentage of red algae (67.1%) reported for the rocky shore flora of the Southern California Bight (Murray and Littler 1989). We found the green seaweeds to occur in slightly lower percentages (7.5% vs 11.3%, respectively) while the percentage of brown seaweeds was very similar (20.2% vs 20.7%, respectively). Our floristic records were also highly comparable to those of Zedler (1976, 1978) who found red seaweeds to comprise 66.3% of the flora, browns 21.7% and greens 9.9%. Red seaweeds (70.9%) also dominated the flora reported by Engle (2005), followed by brown (21.8%), and green (9.9%) algae. Gerrard's (2005) records for her five Palos Verdes sites revealed that red seaweeds constituted 74.3% of the peninsula intertidal flora, brown seaweeds 17.6%, and green seaweeds 5.4%.

The best compilation of the marine algae and seagrasses of San Diego County is contained in Stewart (1991). We identified two macrophytes that were not listed by Stewart (1991) in her analysis of the flora of the entire County region. These were the red seaweeds: *Caulacanthus ustulatus* and *Dasya binghamiae*. *Caulacanthus ustulatus* is believed to be a recent introduction to the southern California marine algal flora and has become very abundant in recent years on many southern California rocky shores (Miller 2004; Murray et al. 2005; Whiteside et al. 2007). At least two other seaweeds (*Sargassum muticum* and *Lomentaria hakodatensis*) also are non-native constituents of the Cabrillo National Monument rocky intertidal flora. *Dasya binghamiae* is the second species of *Dasya* to be recognized as part of the San Diego County flora, joining *Dasya sinicola* var *abyssicola* and *D. sinicola* var. *californica*. However, both *C. ustulatus* and *D. binghamiae* appeared in the list reported by Engle (2005).

As pointed out, difficulties exist in comparing the macrophyte records obtained during our study with previous surveys of the Cabrillo National Monument shoreline (Zedler, 1976, 1978; Engle 2005). Conservatively, we believe that a minimum of 33 taxa (2 green, 5 brown, and 26 red seaweeds) found during our study were not reported for the Cabrillo National Monument flora by Zedler (1976, 1978); drift specimens are not included in this tally (Table 2). Based on their common occurrence at many other southern California sites, the most noteworthy of the greens and browns not reported by Zedler (1976, 1978) include *Chaetomorpha spiralis*, *Colpomenia tuberculata*, *Scytosiphon dotyi*, and *Zonaria farlowii*. Of the 27 red seaweeds, *Ahnfeltiopsis leptophylla*, *Amphiroa beauvoisii*, *Callophyllis violacea*, *Caulacanthus ustulatus*, *Chondracanthus spinosus*, *Cryptopleura violacea*, *Dasya binghamiae*, *Erythroglossum californicum*, *Gelidium purpurascens*, *Gymnogongrus chiton*, *Hypnea variabilis*, *Laurencia masonii*, *Lomentaria hakodatensis*, *Porphyra perforata*, *Priontis linearis*, *Schizymenia pacifica*, and *Spyridia filamentosa* were the most notable of the newly reported species. Of these seaweeds, *Chaetomorpha spiralis*, *Ahnfeltiopsis leptophylla*, *Amphiroa beauvoisii*, *Caulacanthus ustulatus*, *Dasya binghamiae*, *Erythroglossum californicum*, *Gymnogongrus chiton*, and *Spyridia filamentosa* appeared in the list reported by Engle (2005). Unfortunately, complete resolution of the macrophyte flora of the Cabrillo National Monument is not possible without access to properly prepared voucher specimens of taxa encountered during previous surveys.

The Southern California Bight has long been known to be a transition zone between warm and cold temperate biogeographic provinces and this is reflected in the species composition of the rocky intertidal floras of the region (Murray and Littler 1981; Murray and Bray 1993). Floras along the northern portions of the Southern California mainland and the westernmost of the Northern Channel Islands tend to have intertidal floras with colder water affinities and are dominated by species also found along the central California coast. Murray and Littler (1981) found these sites to have seaweed floras with 90.2% to 98.4% of their species in common with the central California flora based on distributional records reported by Abbott and Hollenberg (1976). In contrast, the intertidal floras of Santa Catalina Island and San Clemente Island, members of the Southern Channel Islands, tend to include species limited in their distributions to the more southern and warmer waters of the Southern California Bight. Because of the presence of these warmer water species, the floras of the sites studied on these islands had only 71.3% to 75.0% of their species in common with central California. The macrophyte floras of the investigated sites located along the more southerly part of the Southern California mainland (from Corona del Mar south) also tend to have more warmer water species, These floras ranged from 74.6% to 84.4% of species in common with the central California flora. Our results for the Cabrillo National Monument indicate that this site supports one of the more warmer-water floras in the Southern California Bight. We calculate a 72.3% overlap in species composition with central California for the Cabrillo National Monument, a value within the range of those calculated by Murray and Littler (1981) for Santa Catalina and San Clemente Islands. In addition, we found 18 of the 26 macrophyte species indicated by Murray and Bray (1993) to characterize rocky intertidal habitats bathed by warmer water in the Southern California Bight. These were the green alga *Chaetomorpha spiralis*, the brown seaweeds *Colpomenia sinuosa, Dictyopteris undulata, Dictyota coriacea (as Pachydictyon coriaceum), Eisenia arborea, Endarachne binghamiae, Stephanocystis dioica, Sargassum agardhianum, Taonia lennebackerae, Zonaria farlowii,* and the red algae *Amphiroa beauvoisii (as Amphiroa zonata), Chondria acrorhizophora (as Chondria californica), Corallina pinnatifolia, Haliptilon roseum (as Haliptylon gracile), Hypnea valentiae, Jania crassa, Lithothrix aspergillum, Osmundea sinicola (as Laurencia sinicola),* and *Pterocladiella capillacea (as Pterocladia capillacea).*

Summary

Our coarse survey of the intertidal macrophytes of the Cabrillo National Monument produced a flora of 94 macrophytes that was numerically dominated by red seaweeds. The number of observed taxa and the degree of red algal dominance was comparable to many other rocky intertidal sites in the Southern California Bight and elsewhere in California. We noted the presence of a minimum of 33 taxa (2 green, 5 brown, and 26 red seaweeds) not previously reported for the exposed, westward-facing rocky intertidal coast of the Cabrillo National Monument. The flora of this rocky shore is unique among sites found along the Southern California mainland because of the high proportion of macrophytes that characterize warmer-water sites in this important biogeographic transition region along the Pacific coast. Unfortunately, detailed records of the floristic history of this site are not available. Previous investigations have been limited and the voucher specimens required to ensure taxonomic accuracy in species identification are not available. Thus, our study, with properly prepared and filed voucher specimens serves as a starting point for following future changes in the composition of the Cabrillo National Monument's intertidal flora. Given the unique biogeographic character and the documented impacts of public use on this southern part of the Point Loma Peninsula, we recommend that floristic surveys (and preferably ecological studies of distribution and abundance) be performed by skilled macrophyte taxonomists at least once every five years. These surveys are necessary to assist managers of the Cabrillo National Monument in their efforts to document changes in the intertidal macrophyte flora brought about by the introduction of non-indigenous species and on-going changes in ocean climate.

Literature Cited

Abbott, I. A., and G. J. Hollenberg. 1976. Marine algae of California. Stanford University Press, Stanford, California.

Craig, M. T., and D. J. Pondella, II. 2006. A Survey of the fishes of the Cabrillo National Monument, San Diego, California. California Fish and Game 92(4) 172-183

Dawson, E. Y. 1959. A primary report on the benthic marine flora of southern California. *In* Oceanographic survey of the continental shelf area of southern California. Publication 20. State Water Pollution Control Board, Sacramento, California.

Dawson, E. Y. 1965. Intertidal algae. *In* An oceanographic and biological survey of the southern California mainland shelf. Publication 27. State Water Quality Control Board, Sacramento, California.

Engle, D. L., and J. Largier. 2006. Assessment of coastal water resources and watershed conditions at Cabrillo National Monument, California. Technical Report NPS/NRWRD/NRTR-2006/355. National Park Service, Water Resources Division, Denver, Colorado.

Engle, J. M. 2005. Rocky intertidal resource dynamics in San Diego County: Cardiff, La Jolla, and Point Loma. Final eight-year report (1997/2005). Marine Science Institute. Cooperative Agreement No. N68711-97-LT-70034. University of California, Santa Barbara.

Engle, J. M., and G. E. Davis. 2000a. Baseline surveys of rocky intertidal ecological resources at Point Loma, San Diego. Open-File Report 00-61. U. S. Geological Survey, Sacramento, California.

Engle, J. M., and G. E. Davis. 2000b. Ecological condition and public use of the Cabrillo National Monument intertidal zone 1990–1995. Open-File Report 00-98. U. S. Geological Survey, Sacramento, California.

Engle, J. M., D. L. Martin, D. Hubbard, and D. Farrar. 2000. Rocky intertidal resource dynamics at Point Loma, San Diego County, California. 1996–1998 Report. MMS OCS Study 2001-016. MMS Cooperative Agreement Number 14-35-0001-30758. Coastal Research Center, Marine Science Institute, University of California, Santa Barbara, California.

Gerrard, A. L. 2005. Changes in the rocky intertidal floras along the Palos Verdes Peninsula (Los Angeles County) since E. Y. Dawson's surveys in the late 1950s. Thesis. California State University, Fullerton, California.

McArdle, D. A. 1997. California Marine Protected Areas. Publication No. T-039. California Sea Grant College System, La Jolla, California.

Miller, K. A. 2004. California's non-native seaweeds. Fremontia 32:10–15.

Murray, S. N., and R. N. Bray. 1993. Benthic macrophytes. Pages 304–368 *in* M. D. Dailey, D. J. Reish, and J. W. Anderson, editors. Ecology of the Southern California Bight: A synthesis and interpretation. University of California Press, Berkeley, California.

Murray, S. N., and M. M. Littler. 1981. Biogeographical analysis of intertidal macrophyte floras of southern California. Journal of Biogeography 8:339–351.

Murray, S. N., and M. M. Littler. 1989. Seaweeds and seagrasses of southern California: Distributional lists for twenty-one rocky intertidal sites. Bulletin of the Southern California Academy of Sciences 88:61–79.

Murray, S. N., R. F. Ambrose, and M. N. Dethier. 2006. Monitoring rocky shores. University of California Press, Berkeley, California.

Murray, S. N., L. Fernandez, and J. A. Zertuche-Gonzalez. 2005. Status, environmental threats, and policy considerations for invasive seaweeds for the Pacific coast of North America. Commission for Environmental Cooperation, Montreal, Canada.

Stewart, J. G. 1991. Marine algae and seagrasses of San Diego County. Report No. T-CSGCP-020. California Sea Grant College, University of California, La Jolla, California.

Whiteside, K. E., J. R. Smith, and S. N. Murray. 2007. Distribution, habitat utilization, and reproductive patterns in *Caulacanthus ustulatus* (Caulacanthaceae, Gigartinales), a newly established seaweed on southern California shores. Bulletin of the Southern California Academy of Sciences 106:89–90.

Zedler, J. B. 1976. Ecological resource inventory of the Cabrillo National Monument intertidal zone. Biology Department, San Diego State University Project Report. National Park Service, Denver, Colorado.

Zedler, J. B. 1978. Public use effects in the Cabrillo National Monument intertidal zone. Biology Department, San Diego State University Project Report. National Park Service, Denver, Colorado.

Appendix: Common and Conspicuous Macroalgae and Sea Grasses

Contents

Chlorophyta

Plate 1. *Chaetomorpha aerea* (Dillwyn) Kützing
Habitat: Middle to high zone, often in shallow pools
Scaling: ~5 X

Plate 2. *Chaetomorpa spiralis* Okamura
Habitat: Low zone in Phyllospadix zone; occasional epiphyte
Scaling: ~1 X

Plate 3. *Codium fragile* ssp. *californicum* (J. Agardh) Maggs
Habitat: Tops and sides of boulders, low zone
Scaling: ~½ X

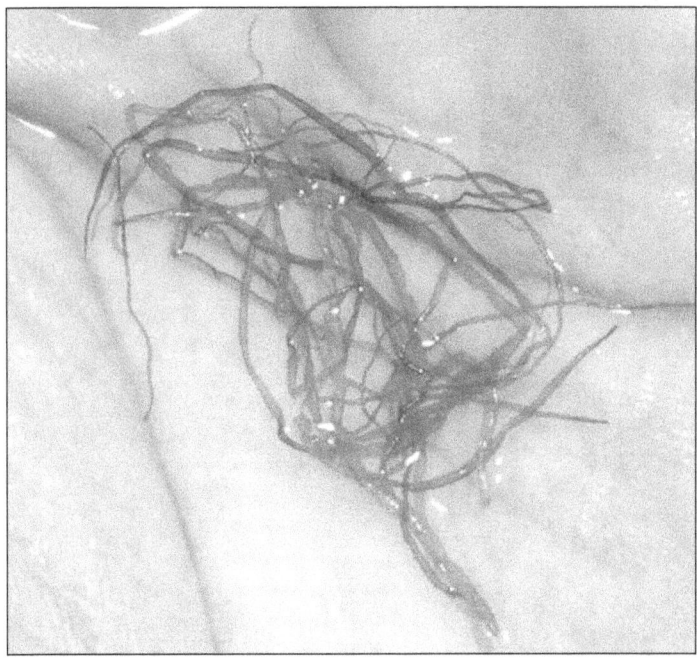

Plate 4. *Ulva* spp. [*Enteromorpha* spp.]
Habitat: Upper shore on damp surfaces
Scaling: 2 X

Plate 5. *Ulva californica* Wille
Habitat: High and middle zone
Scaling: ~3 X

Heterokontophyta (Class Phaeophyceae)

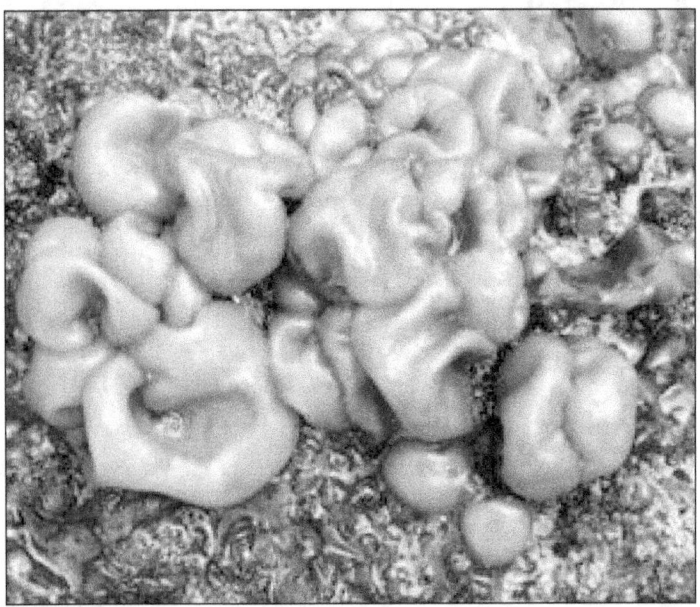

Plate 6. *Colpomenia sinuosa* (Merten ex Roth) Derbès & Solier
Habitat: Mid to low zone; growing in coralline turf
Scaling: ~1 X

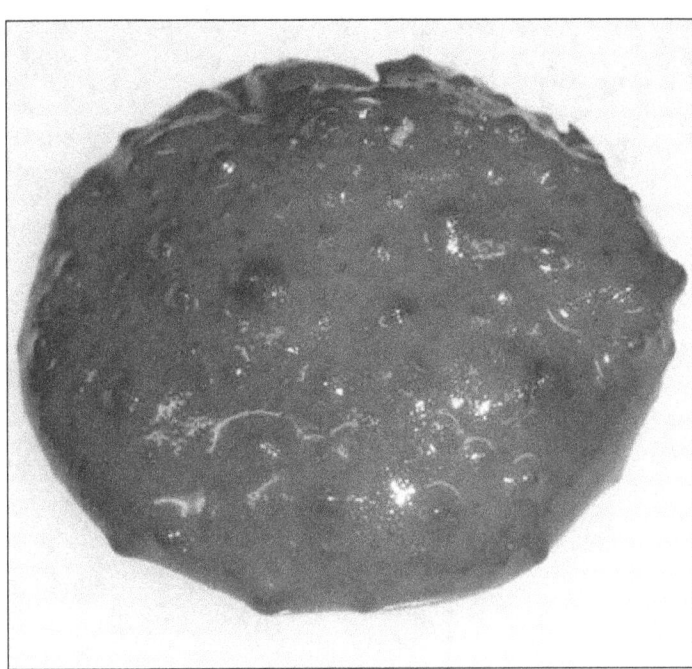

Plate 7. *Colpomenia tuberculata* Saunders
Habitat: Epiphytic on coralline turf
Scaling: ~1 ¼ X

Plate 8. *Dictyopteris undulata* Holmes
Habitat: Low to subtidal zones
Scaling: ~ ½ X

Plate 9. *Dictyota coriacea* (Holmes) Hwang, H.S. Kim & W.J. Lee
Habitat: Low zone to subtidal; occasional mid-zone pools
Scaling: ~ ¾ X

Plate 10. *Egregia menziesii* (Turner) Areschoug
Adult and juvenile (lower left) thalli
Habitat: Low zone
Scaling: Adult thalli ~ 1/15 X

Plate 11. *Eisenia arborea* Areschoug
Habitat: Low zone
Scaling: ~ 1/10 X

Plate 12. *Endarachne binghamiae* J. Agardh
Habitat: High and middle zones
Scaling: ~1 X

Plate 13. *Petrospongium rugosum* (Okamura) Setchell & Gardner
Habitat: High to middle zone
Scaling: ~2 X

Plate 14. *Pseudolithoderma nigrum* Hollenberg
Habitat: High zone (black crust)
Scaling: ~ ½ X

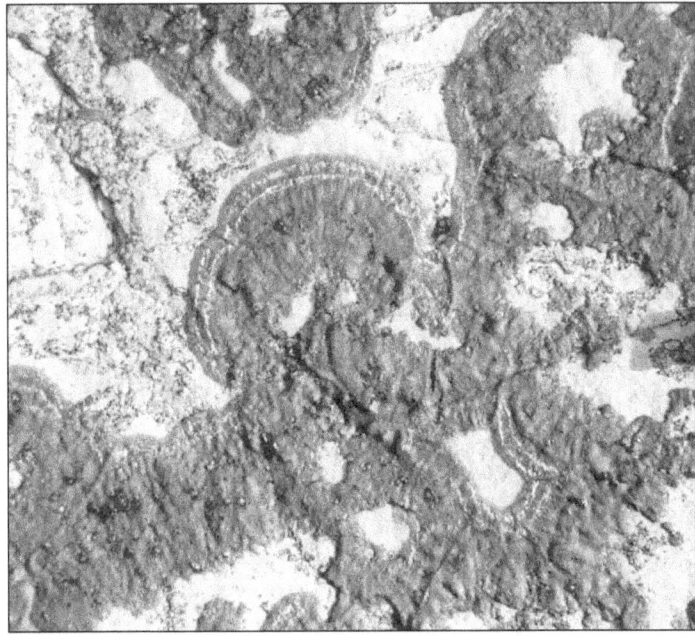

Plate 15. *Ralfsia* spp.
Habitat: High zone
Scaling: ~1 X

Plate 16. *Sargassum agardhianum* Farlow
Habitat: Low zone
Scaling: ~ ¼ X

Plate 17. *Sargassum muticum* (Yendo) Fenscholt
Habitat: Middle and low zone in pools; subtidal
Scaling: ~ ¼ X

Plate 18. *Scytosiphon dotyi* Wynne
Habitat: Upper zone
Scaling: ~ ¼ X

Plate 19. *Silvetia compressa* (J.Agardh) Serrão, Cho, Boo, & Brawley
Habitat: Middle zone
Scaling: ~ ½ X

Plate 20. *Stephanocystis dioica* (Gardner) Draisma, Ballesteros Rousseau, & Thibaut
Habitat: Low zone
Scaling: ~ ⅓ X

Plate 21. *Taonia lennebackerae* J. Agardh
Habitat: Low zone, common in sand-influenced areas
Scaling: ~ ¾ X

Plate 22. *Zonaria farlowii* Setchell & Gardner
Habitat: Middle and low zone pools and subtidal; common in sand-influenced areas
Scaling: ~ ⅓

Rhodophyta

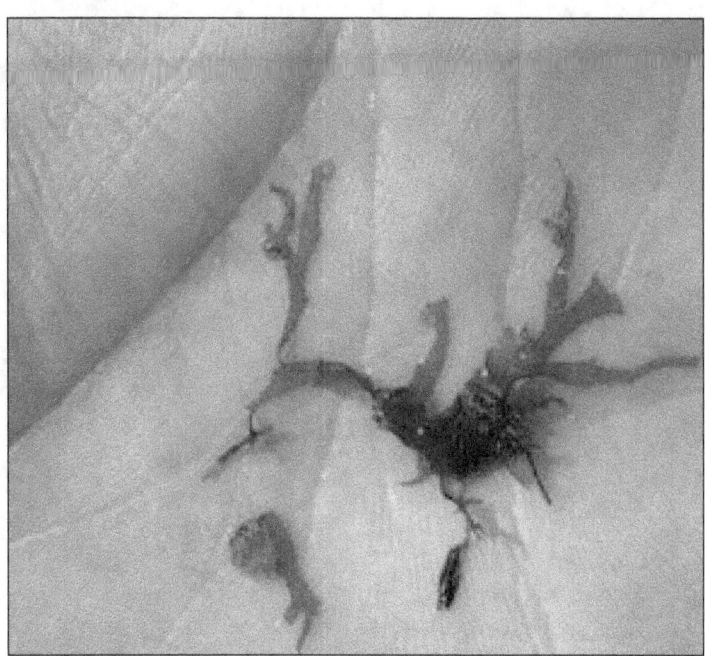

Plate 23. *Acrosorium ciliolatum* (Harvey) Kylin
Habitat: Low zone on rocks or epiphytic on other seaweeds, particularly corallines
Scaling: ~2 X

Plate 24. *Amphiroa beauvoisii* Lamouroux
Habitat: Low zone; tidepools
Scaling: See scale

Plate 25. *Bossiella dichotoma* (Manza) P.C. Silva
Habitat: Low and subtidal zones; tidepools
Scaling: ~ ⅓ X

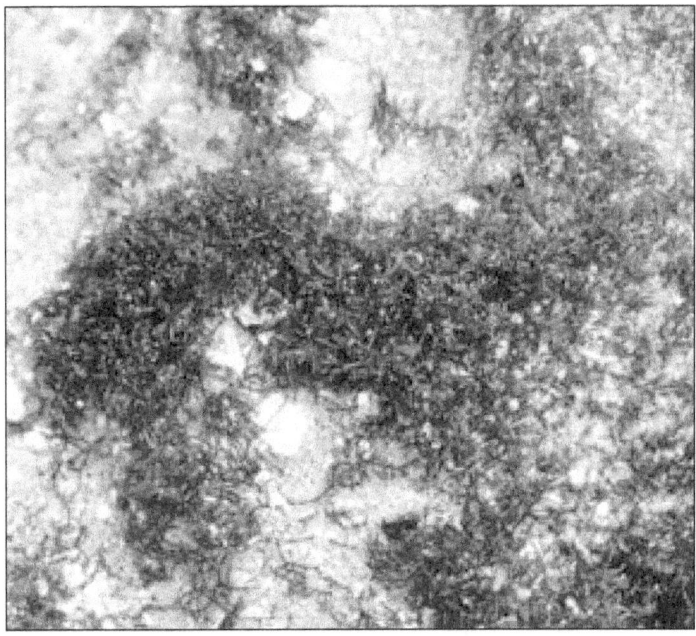

Plate 26. *Caulacanthus ustulatus* (Mertens ex Turner) Kützing
Habitat: High and middle zones; growing on rock, *Silvetia*, mussels and other organisms
Scaling: ~4 X

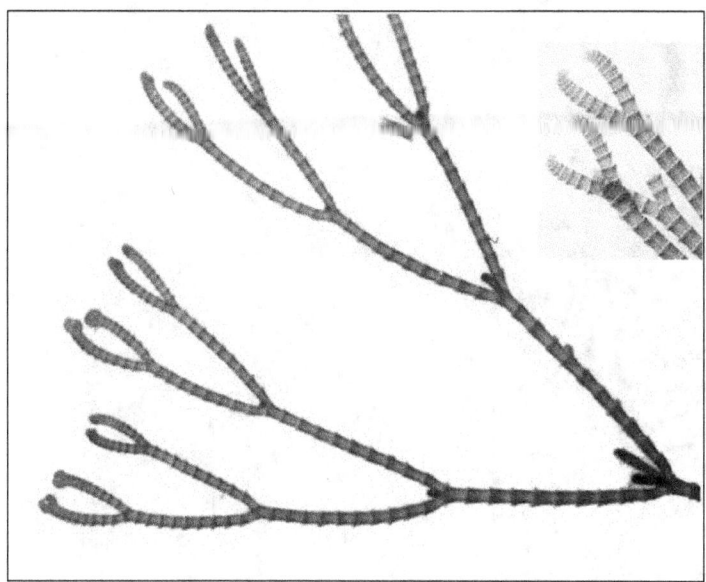

Plate 27. *Centroceras clavulatum* (C. Agardh) Montagne
Habitat: Middle zone turf
Scaling: ~10 X

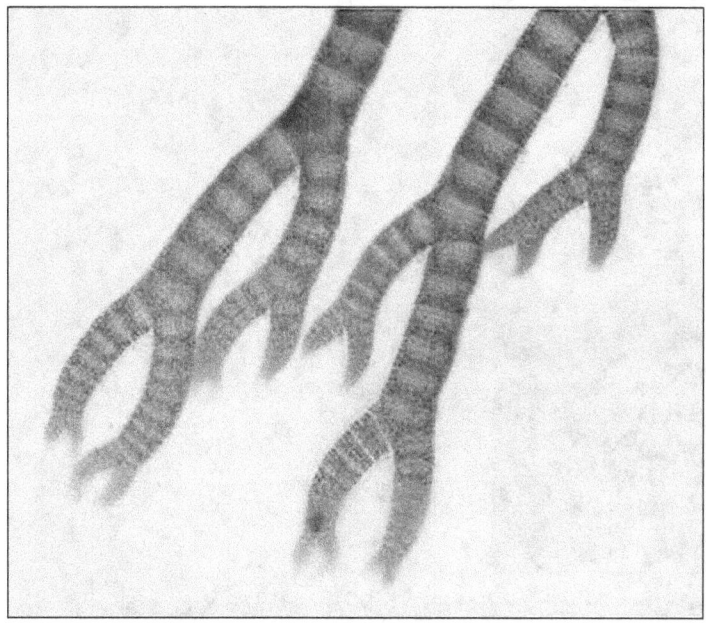

Plate 28. *Ceramium sinicola* Stetchell & Gardner
Habitat: Middle zone turf; can be epiphytic including on *Codium*
Scaling: ~12

Plate 29. *Chondracanthus canaliculatus* (Harvey) Guiry in Hommersand, Guiry, Fredericq & Leister
Habitat: Common in middle zone; under *Silvetia* and in pools and crevices
Scaling: ~ ¾ X

Plate 30. *Chondracanthus spinosus* (Kützing) Guiry in Hommersand, Guiry, Fredericq & Leister
Habitat: Middle and low zone; under *Silvetia* or sides of rocks in pools
Scaling: ~2 X

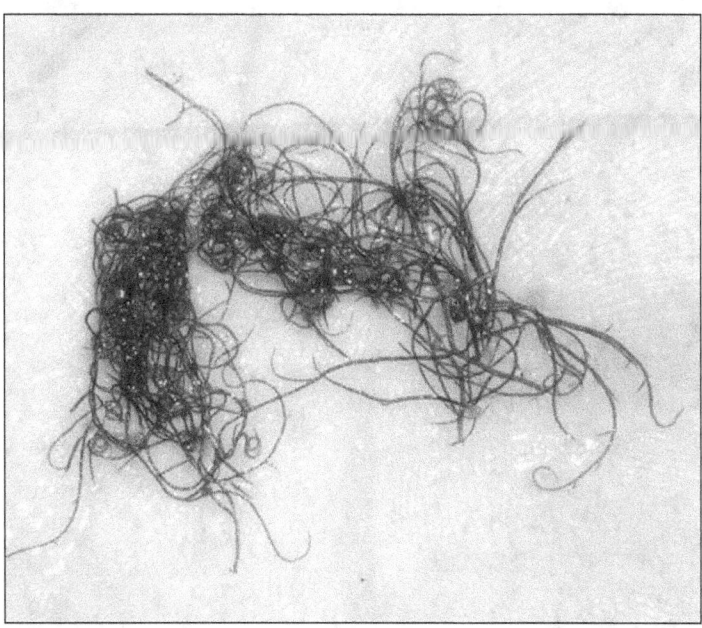

Plate 31. *Chondria acrorhizophora* Setchell & Gardner
Habitat: Mid intertidal pools to low zone; epiphytic on *Phyllospadix*
Scaling: ~2 X

Plate 32. *Corallina chilensis* Decaisne
Habitat: Low zone; in tide pools and under *Phyllospadix*
Scaling: ~1 ¼ X

Plate 33. *Corallina pinnatifolia* (Manza) Dawson
Habitat: Middle and low zone coralline turfs
Scaling: ~1 ¼ X

Plate 34. *Corallina vancouveriensis* Yendo
Habitat: Middle and low zone coralline turfs
Scaling: ~1 X

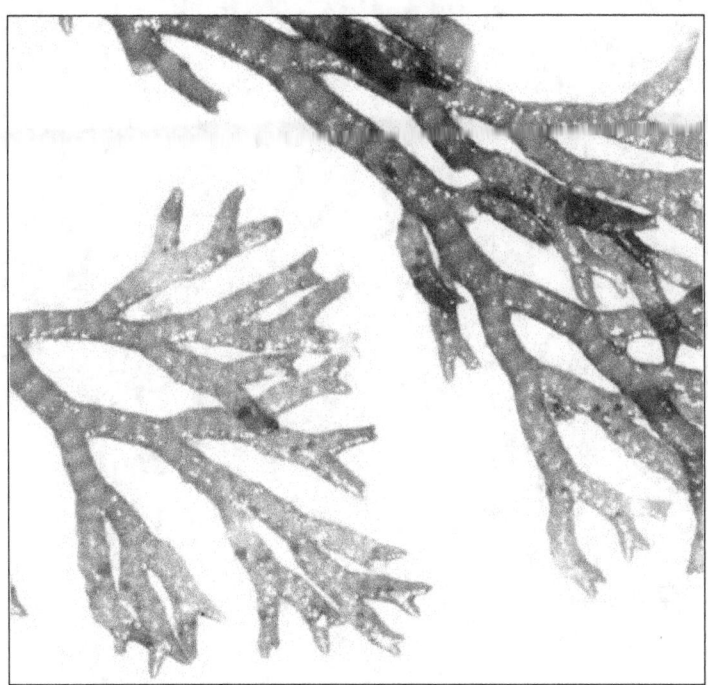

Plate 35. *Corallophila eatoniana* (Farlow) T.O. Cho, Choi, G.I. Hansen & Boo
Habitat: Middle zone turf; along the edges of pools
Scaling: ~10 X

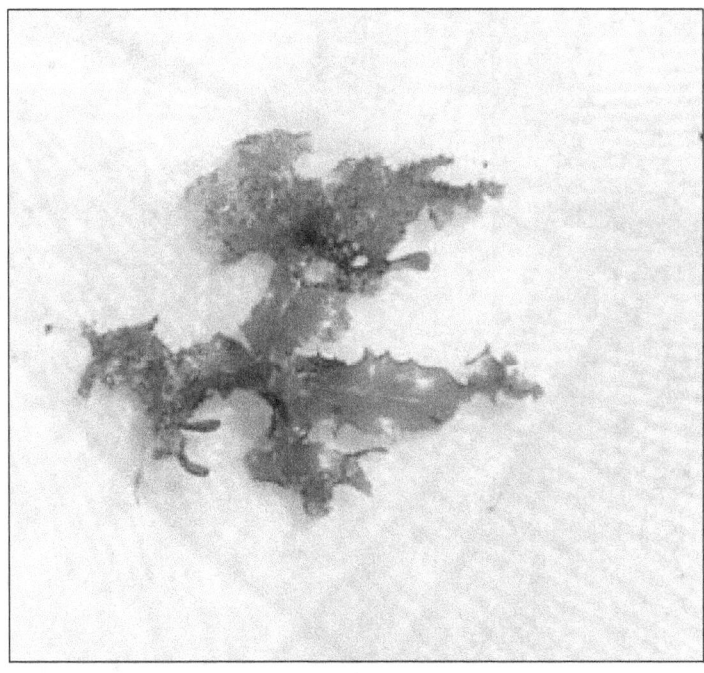

Plate 36. *Cryptopleura crispa* Kylin
Habitat: Epiphytic on corallines and other algae
Scaling: ~2 ½ X

Plate 37. *Cryptopleura violacea* (J. Agardh) Kylin
Habitat: Subtidal zone
Scaling: See scale

Plate 38. *Cumagloia andersonii* (Farlow) Setchell & Gardner
Habitat: High and middle zones
Scaling: ~ ⅓ X

Plate 39. *Erythrocystis saccata* (J. Agardh) Silva
Habitat: Epiphytic on *Laurencia pacifica*
Scaling: ~2 ½ X

Plate 40. *Gastroclonium parvum* (Hollenberg) Chang & Xia
Habitat: Middle and low zone turfs; epiphytic
Scaling: ~2 X

Plate 41. *Gelidum coulteri* Harvey
Habitat: High and middle zones; occasional in pools
Scaling: ~3 X

Plate 42. *Gelidium purpurascens* Gardner
Habitat: Low zone
Scaling: ~ ⅓ X

Plate 43. *Gelidium pusillum* (Stackhouse) LeJolie
Habitat: Middle zone turf; occasional epiphytes on snails
Scaling: ~1 ¼ X

Plate 44. *Gelidium robustum* (Gardner) Hollenberg & Abbott
Habitat: Low zone
Scaling: ~ ½

Plate 45. *Haliptilon roseum* (Lamarck) D.J. Garbary & H.W. Johansen
Habitat: In pools in low zone
Scaling: See scale

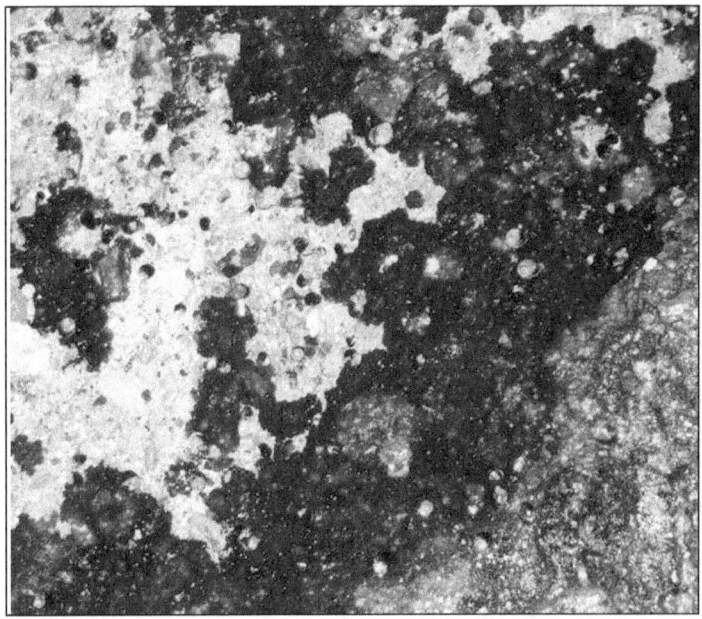

Plate 46. *Hildenbrandia* sp.
Habitat: High zones, especially in pools
Scaling: ~ ½ X

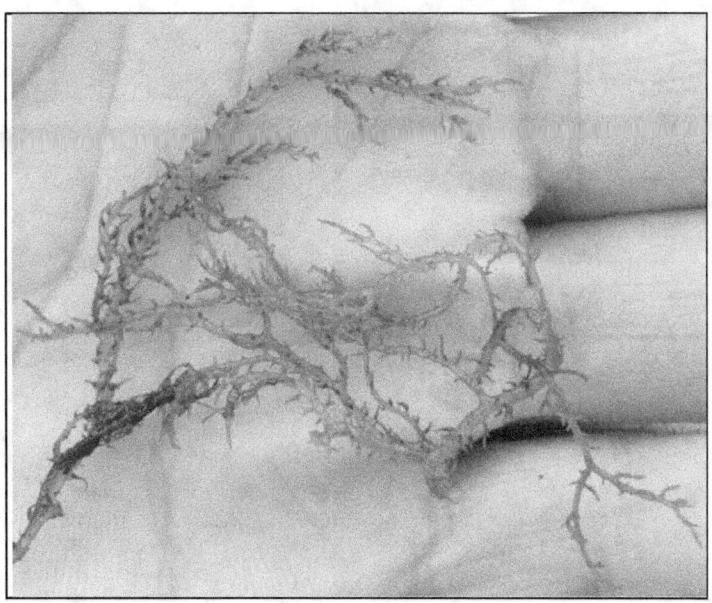

Plate 47. *Hypnea valentiae* (Turner) Montagne
Habitat: Middle to low zones; occasional epiphyte
Scaling: ~1 X

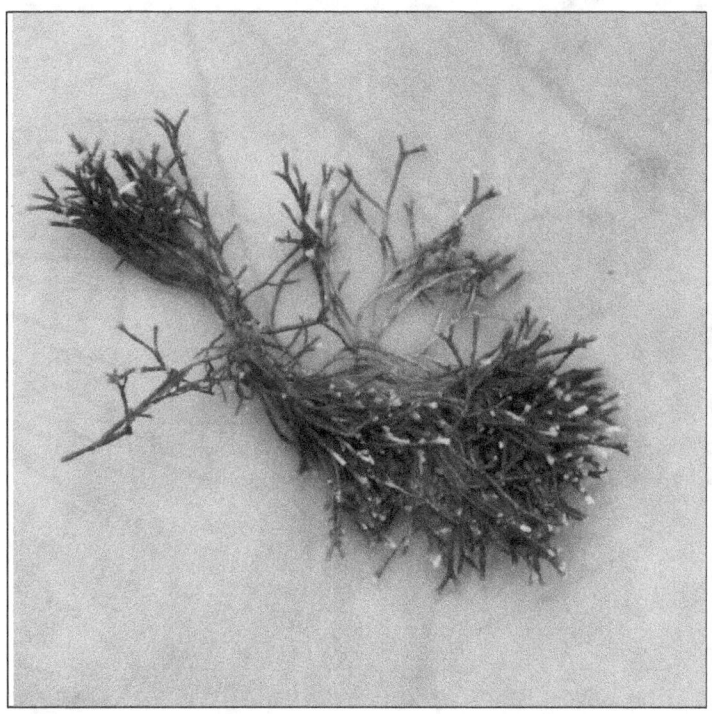

Plate 48. *Jania crassa* Lamouroux
Habitat: Middle and low zones; in pools
Scaling: ~2 X

Plate 49. *Laurencia masonii* Setchell & Gardner
Habitat: Low to subtidal zone
Scaling: See scale

Plate 50. *Laurencia pacifica* Kylin
Habitat: Middle and low zones
Scaling: ~1 X

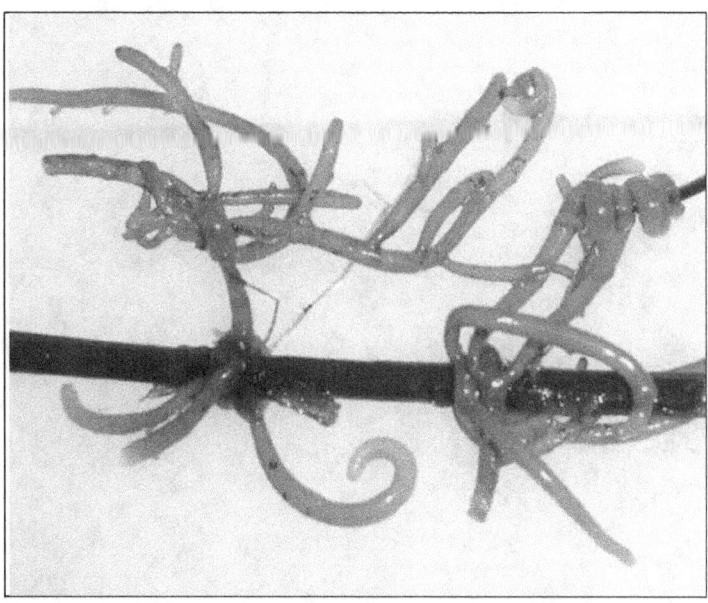

Plate 51. *Laurencia subopposita* (J.Agrdh) Setchell
Habitat: Low zone; epiphytic on other seaweed and *Phyllospadix*
Scaling: ~2 X

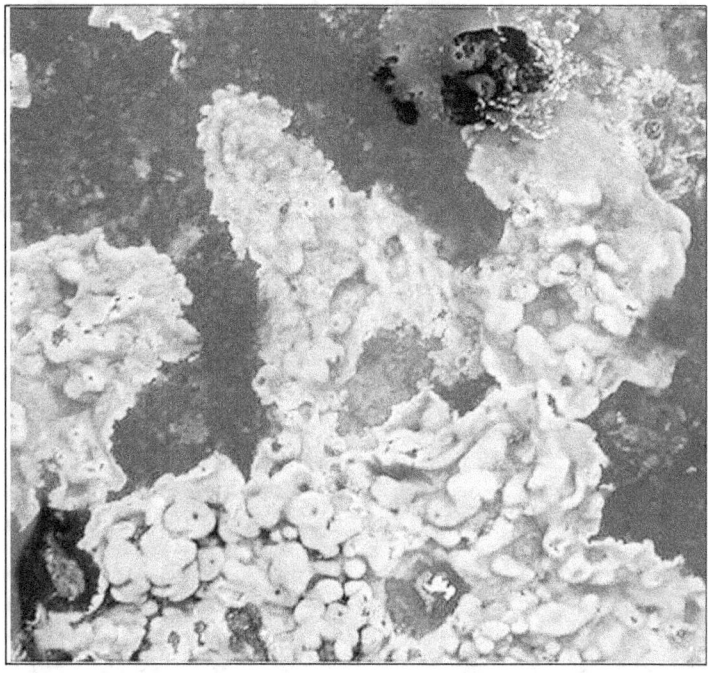

Plate 52. *Lithophyllum neofarlowii* Stechell & Mason
Habitat: High zone; in crevices
Scaling: ~2 X

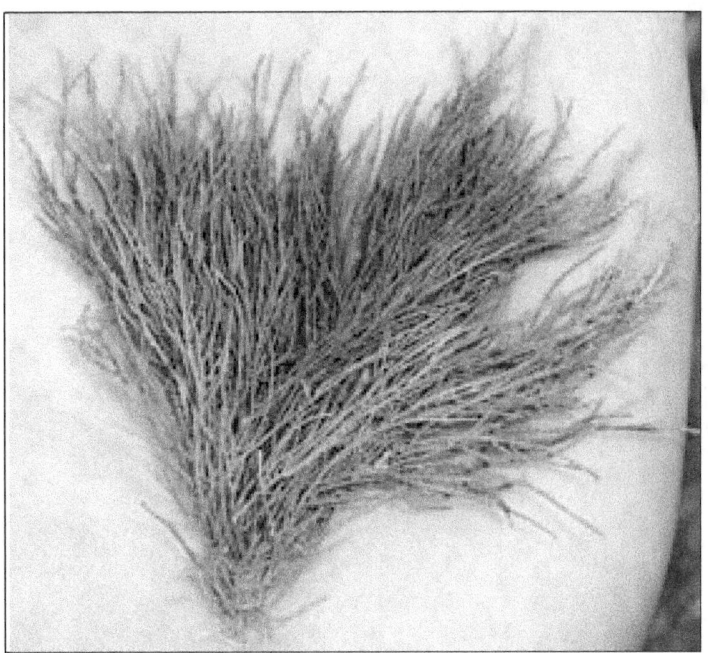

Plate 53. *Lithothrix aspergillum* Gray
Habitat: Low zone in pools and turf
Scaling: ~1 X

Plate 54. *Lomentaria hakodatensis* Yendo
Habitat: Middle zone turfs
Scaling: ~2 X

Plate 55. *Mazzaella affinis* (Harvey) Fredericq in Hommersand, Guiry, Fredericq & Leister
Habitat: Middle and low zones
Scaling: ~1 ½ X

Plate 56. *Mazzaella leptorhynchos* (J. Agardh) Leister in Hommersand, Guiry, Fredericq & Leister
Habitat: Middle and low zones
Scaling: ~ ½ X

Plate 57. *Melobesia* spp.
Habitat: Low zone; epiphytic on *Phyllospadix*
Scaling: ~2 X

Plate 58. *Neogastroclonium subarticulatum* (Turner) Le Gall, Dalen & G. W. Saunders
Habitat: Low zone
Scaling: ~1 X

Plate 59. *Nienburgia andersoniana* (J. Agardh) Kylin
Habitat: Low zone
Scaling: ¾ X

Plate 60. *Osmundea sinicola* (Setchell & Gardner) Nam
Habitat: Middle zone turfs
Scaling: ~ ½ X

Plate 61. *Osmundea spectabilis* var. *dieogensis* (Dawson) Nam
Habitat: Low zone
Scaling: ~ ½ X

Plate 62. *Plocamium pacificum* Kylin
Habitat: Low zone in pools or under *Phyllospadix*
Scaling: ~ ½ X

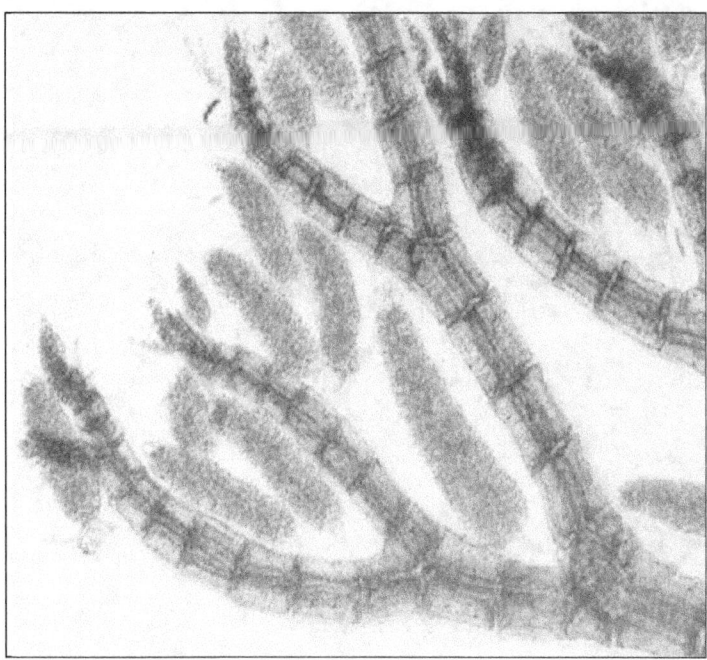

Plate 63. *Polysiphonia* spp.
Habitat: Upper, Middle, and Low zones
Scaling: ~20 X

Plate 64. *Porphyra* spp.
Habitat: High zone
Scaling: ~1 X

Plate 65. *lanceolata* (Harvey) Harvey
Habitat: Low zone
Scaling: ~1 X

Plate 66. *Pterocladiella capillacea* (S.G. Gmelin) Santelices & Hommersand
Habitat: Low zone; occasional middle zone in pools
Scaling: ~1 X

Plate 67. *Pterosiphonia baileyi* (Harvey) Falkenberg
Habitat: Low zone; occasional in middle zone turf
Scaling: ~3 X

Plate 68. *Pterosiphonia dendroidea* (Montagne) Falkenberg
Habitat: Low zone, especially under *Phyllospadix* in sand
Scaling: See scale

Plate 69. *Rhodymenia californica* Kylin
Habitat: Low zone to subtidal
Scaling: ~ ½ X

Plate 70. *Rhodymenia pacifica* Kylin
Habitat: Low zone
Scaling: ~1 ½

Plate 71. *Smithora naiadum* (Anderson) Hollenberg
Habitat: Epiphytic on *Phyllospadix*
Scaling: ~3 X

Spermatophyta

Plate 72. *Phyllospadix torreyi* Watson
Habitat: Low zone
Scaling: ~$\frac{1}{10}$ X

NPS 342/109342, August 2011